To John
in recollection
of joyful hours
of looking and
talking!
Arthur

THE ISABELLA STEWART GARDNER MUSEUM

TITIAN'S
RAPE
OF
EUROPA

TITIANI VECELLII PICTORIS CELEBERRIMI AC
FAMOSISSIMI VERA EFFIGIES.

ILL.ᵐᵒ ET R.ᵐᵒ D. Dᴺᵒ HENRICO CAETANO S.R.E. CARD. AMPL.ᵐᵒ BON.ᵉⁿ LEGATO
EXIGVVM HOC MVNVS IMAGINIS TITIANI PICT. CVIVS NOMEN ORBIS CONTINERE NON VALET SVB MISSE DICAT SACRATQVE
HVMILL.ᵐᵉ DEDIT.ᵠ D. SERVVS AVGVST. CARRATIVS. 1587

Published *for* THE ISABELLA STEWART GARDNER MUSEUM

TITIAN'S RAPE OF EUROPA

A STUDY OF THE COMPOSITION AND THE MODE OF REPRESENTATION IN THIS AND RELATED PAINTINGS

by Arthur Pope

by HARVARD UNIVERSITY PRESS, Cambridge, Massachusetts, 1960

Distributed in Great Britain by Oxford University Press, London

Typography by Burton J Jones

Composition and color plate section
by Harvard University Printing Office, Cambridge, Massachusetts

Lithographed in the U.S.A. by Meriden Gravure Company, Meriden, Connecticut

Bound by Stanhope Bindery, Inc., Boston, Massachusetts

Library of Congress Catalog Card Number 60–11562

PREFACE

Visitors to the Gardner Museum frequently ask why Titian's painting, "The Rape of Europa," is considered such an outstanding masterpiece. This small book is an attempt to give at least a partial answer to that question. It might be enough simply to stress the high regard in which Titian has always been held by artists, connoisseurs, and collectors in his own and the following centuries, and to consider the place occupied by the "Europa" in relation to the development of his art as a whole. One could emphasize its significance in revealing the taste and interests of the late Renaissance in Venice and in the rest of Europe. But it is the especial aim of this brief essay to suggest something of the qualities to be discerned in the painting itself so that, by anyone seeing it today, it may be understood and above all enjoyed, even though, as in watching the performance of a Shakespeare play, one may give little thought at the moment as to precise sources and history.

The book is addressed primarily to the visitor to the Museum who is thus able to see the picture itself. To others it is hoped that the plates may convey something of its finer qualities as well as its general aspect. The colored reproduction that serves as frontispiece gives a useful approximation of the superficial effect. But it must be remembered that even the best printed reproduction in color is actually a transposition into a palette quite different from that of the painter's, and also that the quality of ink on paper is unlike that of paint of varying thicknesses on canvas. The color and quality, therefore, must be taken with reservations.

It is impossible to tell where all one's ideas come from; but I owe much to conversations and discussions with innumerable pupils and colleagues extending over many years of active teaching. For their stimulating interest and enduring friendship I am ever grateful. In the present instance, for valuable criticism and suggestions I am particularly indebted to Morton C. Bradley Jr., Professor James M. Carpenter, and Professor Winthrop O. Judkins, as well as to George L. Stout, the Director of the Gardner Museum, who suggested the book in the first place, and who has shown *the utmost patience in response to constant calls for advice and assistance. For ever ready and cheerful help in locating books and photographs I am, like so many others, indebted to Miss Louise Lucas and her staff in the library of the Fogg Art Museum. Also I wish to thank Mrs. Alan Lebowitz of Harvard University Press for valuable suggestions and painstaking care in the editing of the manuscript.*

To many persons and institutions I am under grateful obligation for permission to reproduce photographs. Individual acknowledgments are to be found accompanying the list of illustrations.

June 1960 A. P.

CONTENTS

Subject of the painting: Passage from Ovid's *Metamorphoses*   1

The painting: Plates   3

Introduction   13

Theme and development   15

Pictorial form   21

Representation and performance — phrasing   35

Color   45

Pictorial form in related paintings   47

Note on Titian's life   53

History of the painting   59

Books suggested for reference   61

vii

ILLUSTRATIONS

Agostino Carracci's engraving of Titian's self-portrait on the title page is reproduced by courtesy of Fogg Art Museum, Harvard University

FIGURE   PAGE

1. CRIVELLI: St. George and the Dragon   16
   Courtesy of Isabella Stewart Gardner Museum, Boston

2. GIORGIONE (or TITIAN): Concert Champêtre   17
   Courtesy of Musée du Louvre, Paris. Photograph by Giraudon

3. TITIAN: Entombment   19
   Courtesy of Musée du Louvre. Photograph by Giraudon

4. TITIAN: Study for painting of The Jealous Husband
   in Scuola del Santo, Padua   20
   Courtesy of the École des Beaux-Arts, Paris. Photograph by Giraudon

5. TITIAN: St. Sebastian   22
   Courtesy of Hermitage Museum, Leningrad

6. RUBENS: Rape of the Daughters of Leucippus   23
   Courtesy of Bayerische Staatsgemäldesammlungen, Munich

7. RAPHAEL: Holy Family   24
   Courtesy of Bayerische Staatsgemäldesammlungen, Munich

8. GIORGIONE: Madonna and Saints. Chiesa di
   San Liberale Abbaziale   25
   Courtesy of Chiesa Arcipretale Abbaziale, Castelfranco
   Photograph by G. Lion, Castelfranco

9. TITIAN: Bacchanal (The Andrians)   26
   Courtesy of Museo del Prado, Madrid. Photograph by Anderson

ix

FIGURE   PAGE

10. TITIAN: Bacchus and Ariadne   27
Courtesy of National Gallery, London. Photograph by Anderson

11. TITIAN: Three Ages   31
Courtesy of the Earl of Ellesmere, St. Boswells, Scotland. Photograph by Annan

12. TITIAN: The Education of Cupid   31
Courtesy of Borghese Gallery, Rome. Photograph by Anderson

13. TITIAN: Diana and Callisto   32
Courtesy of the Earl of Ellesmere, St. Boswells, Scotland. Photograph by Annan

14. TINTORETTO: Allegory of Fidelity   37
Courtesy of Fogg Art Museum, Cambridge, Mass.

15. TITIAN: Venus and Cupid   39
Courtesy of Uffizi Gallery, Florence. Photograph by Anderson

16. MANET: Olympia   39
Courtesy of the Musée du Louvre, Paris. Photograph by Giraudon

17. RUBENS: Free Copy of Titian's Bacchanal   42
Courtesy of Nationalmuseum, Stockholm

18. TITIAN: Bacchanal (The Andrians)   43
Courtesy of Museo del Prado, Madrid. Photograph by Anderson

19. TITIAN: Venus of Urbino   46
Courtesy of Uffizi Gallery, Florence. Photograph by Alinari

20. PALMA VECCHIO: Venus   46
Courtesy of Staatliche Kunstsammlungen, Dresden. Photograph by Deutsche Fotothek Dresden

21. CATENA: Warrior Adoring Christ Child   48
Courtesy of National Gallery, London

22. CRANACH: Nymph of the Spring   49
Courtesy of Museum der Bildenden Künste, Leipzig

23. VAN SCOREL: Cleopatra   49
     Courtesy of Rijksmuseum, Amsterdam

24. VERONESE: The Rape of Europa   50
     Courtesy of Palazzo Ducale, Venice. Photograph by Anderson

25. VERONESE: Alexander and the Family of Darius   51
     Courtesy of National Gallery, London

26. DEGAS: Femme au Tub   52
     Courtesy of Hill-Stead Museum, Farmington, Conn.
     Photograph by W. F. Miller and Co.

TITIAN'S

RAPE
OF
EUROPA

THE SUBJECT OF THE PAINTING AS TOLD BY OVID (43 B.C.–17 A.D.)

MERCURY . . . *left the land of Pallas behind him, and flew to heaven on out-flung pinions. Here his father calls him aside; and not revealing his love affair as the real reason, he says: "My son, always faithful to perform my bidding, delay not, but swiftly in accustomed flight glide down to earth and seek out the land that looks up at your mother's star from the left. The natives call it the land of Sidon. There you are to drive down to the sea-shore the herd of the king's cattle which you will see grazing at some distance on the mountain-side." He spoke, and quickly the cattle were driven from the mountain and headed for the shore, as Jove had directed, to a spot where the great king's daughter was accustomed to play in company with her Tyrian maidens. Majesty and love do not go well together, nor tarry long in the same dwelling-place. And so the father and ruler of the gods, who wields in his right hand the three-forked lightning, whose nod shakes the world, laid aside his royal majesty along with his sceptre, and took upon him the form of a bull. In this form he mingled with the cattle, lowed like the rest, and wandered around, beautiful to behold, on the young grass. His colour was white as the untrodden snow, which has not yet been melted by the rainy south-wind. The muscles stood rounded upon his neck, a long dewlap hung down in front; his horns were small, but perfect in shape as if carved by an artist's hand, cleaner and more clear than pearls. His brow and eyes would inspire no fear, and his whole expression was peaceful. Agenor's daughter looked at him in wondering admiration, because he was so beautiful and friendly. But, although he seemed so gentle, she was afraid at first to touch him. Presently she drew near, and held out flowers to his snow-white lips. The disguised lover rejoiced, and, as a foretaste of future joy, kissed her hands. Even so he could scarce restrain his passion. And now he jumps sportively about on the grass, now lays his snowy body down on the yellow sands; and when her fear has little by little been allayed, he yields his breast for her maiden*

1

hands to pat and his horns to entwine with garlands of fresh flowers. The princess even dares to sit upon his back, little knowing upon whom she rests. The god little by little edges away from the dry land, and sets his borrowed hoofs in the shallow water; then he goes further out and soon is in full flight with his prize on the open ocean. She trembles with fear and looks back at the receding shore, holding fast a horn with one hand and resting the other on the creature's back. And her fluttering garments stream behind her in the wind.[1]

[1] Ovid, *Metamorphoses,* with an English translation by Frank Justus Miller (Cambridge, 1916), I, 119–121 (Book 2, lines 833–875, in the Latin).

Dimensions: 70 × 80½ in.

3

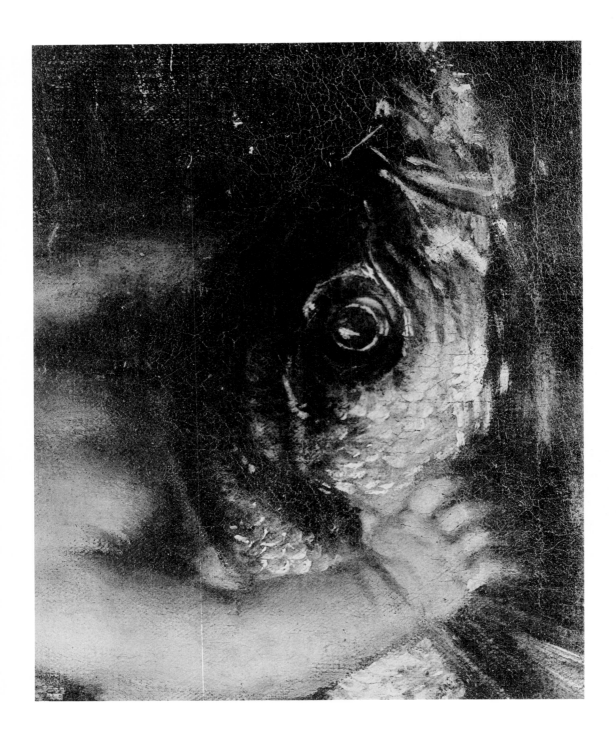

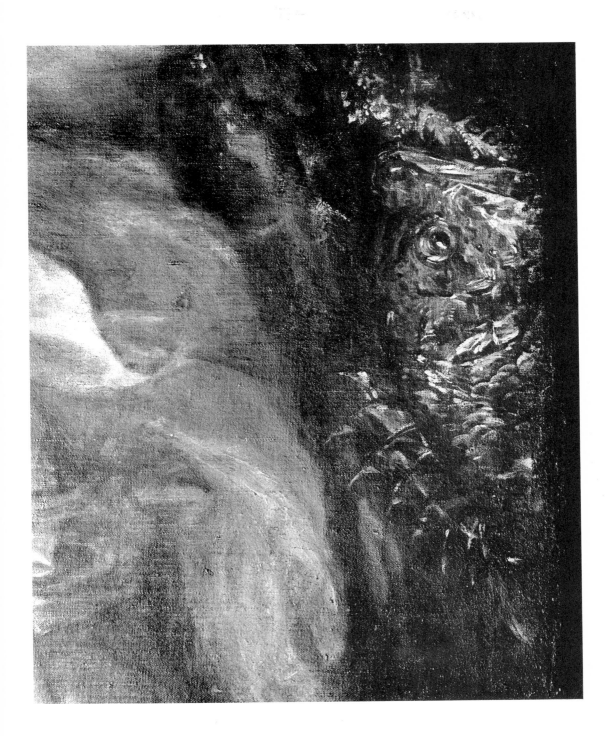

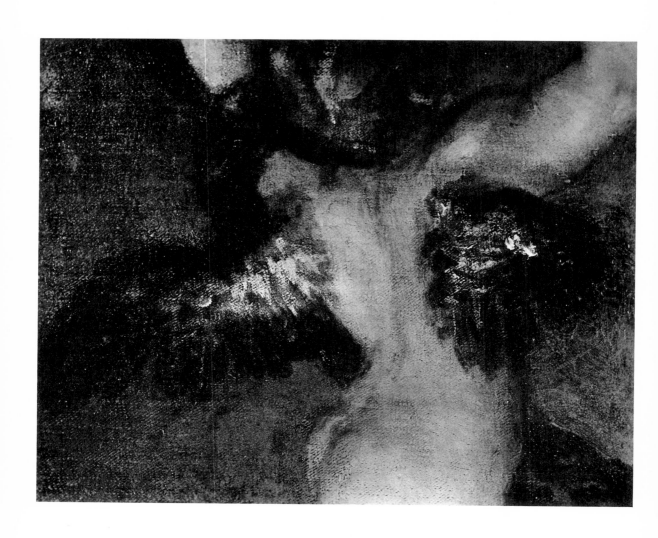

10

INTRODUCTION

THE "Europa" is one of a series of mythological subjects, or "poesies," painted by Titian in the fifteen-fifties and sixties for Philip II of Spain, to decorate the walls of the royal palace in Madrid. Since then, in its various moves from owner to owner and from place to place, it has been one of the most famous paintings of the High Renaissance and has been generally recognized as one of the finest examples of Venetian painting of the sixteenth century. While it was still in Madrid in the winter of 1628–29, Rubens, who seems to have made the most of every opportunity to copy Titian's paintings, made a full-size copy of it, and, according to legend, he called it the first painting in the world. Today even the casual visitor to the Museum [1] can hardly fail to be impressed by its illusion of space and of exuberant action, or to be pleased with its rich color and its effectiveness as tapestry-like decoration.

That, however, is only part of the story, and it is easily possible that the observer, passing on to the next object of interest, may, for one thing, be a bit puzzled as to why the picture is considered so unusual, and he may perhaps, in any case, overlook some of the qualities which give the painting its real significance as one of the world's great masterpieces. Most Renaissance paintings, rather than being designed to be effective for the comparatively quick look that one now is apt to give to pictures in an exhibition or even in a museum, were intended to be lived with, to be seen day after day with increasing pleasure and satisfaction; and the patrons for whom they were painted were on the whole discriminating connoisseurs brought up in an environment in which an understanding and enjoyment of the arts of building, sculpture, and painting, of music and letters, were part of their daily life. Moreover, the subjects themselves, drawn from classical literature, had a vital interest for the noble and royal patrons, and for the humanist scholars of their courts, that is difficult for us to appreciate when

[1] Unless otherwise specified, "the Museum" always refers to the Isabella Stewart Gardner Museum.

13

many of the themes have with constant repetition become so hackneyed. Naturally, then, to get full enjoyment from a painting like the "Europa" today, one should, as much as possible, assume the point of view of a patron of the Renaissance and be ready to study it as one would a piece of poetry or a play, as if one had it in one's own possession to be seen again and again.

To call attention to some of the details which might be overlooked in casual observation, separate photographs of these are shown in the Plates. They emphasize the interest and beauty to be found in particular portions. A music critic in discussing an extended composition often plays over selected passages in isolation to bring out their special meaning. Here the photographs of details serve much the same purpose.

In addition, while bearing in mind that nothing said or put down in words can take the place of looking at the object itself — it is told that Brahms said to the critic, "If what I write does not speak to your heart, I do not care what your head says about it" — nevertheless, just as program notes by the music critic sometimes have their use, it may be helpful to try to explain something of the way in which a painting like this is put together, how its themes are developed, how it is organized within its enframement, and to consider the actual performance on which, as in music, its final quality depends.

The remarks which follow are conceived as those which might be made in conversation with one's friends while standing in front of the picture. As would be natural in such a case, reference is made to other paintings by Titian as well as to some by other masters when this seems to be useful in explaining the general point of view underlying this and other works produced at about the same time.

THEME AND DEVELOPMENT

IT will be useful, first of all, to speculate on how, once having decided to paint the picture, Titian went to work. The subject was probably chosen from among various mythological subjects of an amorous nature suggested by Philip to suit his personal taste. These were of course familiar to both Titian and the king through the writings of classical authors. For the "Europa" Titian evidently turned to Ovid's *Metamorphoses*, and, since Titian has followed Ovid's account pretty closely, even to catching much of its comedy spirit, a translation of the pertinent passage in the *Metamorphoses* is printed above as a proper introduction to the picture. The myth itself presented elements which were simple enough: Europa, daughter of King Agenor, Jupiter in the guise of a bull playfully crowned with a chaplet of flowers, a few *Amorini,* and sea, sky, and landscape background. One can imagine how a Venetian painter of the fifteenth century would have used these elements to make a charming fairy story in a manner suggested by Crivelli's "St. George and the Dragon" in the Raphael Room of the Museum (fig. 1). Or, if one thinks of the "Concert Champêtre" in the Louvre of 1510 or thereabouts (fig. 2), one can fancy the lyrical treatment which Giorgione, or Titian himself, would have given the subject in the early years of the sixteenth century.

By the time of the "Europa," however, some fifty years later, Venetian painting and especially Titian's had become highly dramatic in character. Moreover, partly following the lead of Michelangelo and Raphael, it was conceived in a grand manner that was appropriate to the style of architecture for which it served as decoration. This meant the representation of the human figure in action on a noble scale with the large and sweeping movement which we now associate with grand opera. It meant especially movement of hands and arms and legs in gestures far removed from those of ordinary life. For Titian, therefore, "The Rape of Europa" became drama on this grand scale, half tragedy, half comedy, much in a Shakespearian vein,, and the figure of Europa posed in wild abandon on the back of the

15

1. CRIVELLI: St. George and the Dragon

2. GIORGIONE (or TITIAN): Concert Champêtre

bull became naturally the main theme of the composition. With head turned back in opposition to the spiral twist of torso and legs, the pose suggests a derivation from those developed by Michelangelo to give vivid expression of passionate feeling. Often referred to as *contrapposto*, these came to be characteristic of the Baroque art of the seventeenth century. In the present instance, the pose, taken together with the broken, or "ragged," silhouette of the whole mass of figure and drapery, gives a foretaste of Baroque style.

Titian now proceeded, very like a composer of music, to develop this central theme embodied in the figure of Europa, or perhaps rather to extend it, by repeats and echoes and allusions reaching into the rest of the

17

design. Of course one cannot tell in what order or how consciously he thought of all these things. Probably, as in any kind of design, the composition was conceived at first roughly as a whole and gradually perfected. We are concerned only with the final result. Accordingly, one may note how the gesture of Europa's upraised arm is repeated and enlarged by the flying red scarf, and that in a similar way the direction of the lower leg is repeated in the brownish drapery which trails in the water below. Down on the left, as a joyful master of ceremonies, the small Amor, or Eros, with legs flying out behind, sails around the corner in pursuit of the main figures — a comedy echo of the pose and action of Europa. To accent this theme still further, the pattern of the Amor's legs is repeated on a smaller scale in the surprising flourish of the end of the bull's tail just above. One can imagine how pleased with himself Titian must have been for this bit of invention, for it evidently was an afterthought; the original, quite different drawing of the tail is now dimly revealed where some of the final surface of paint in the course of time has been rubbed off. Moreover, the whole desperate action of Europa seems repeated in the tossing of the hills and mountains in the distance, while the pose of the central Amor above is close to an inversion of that of Europa. By such means the action of the figure is so extended and enlarged that it seems to fill the whole canvas.

Similar repeats of themes by minor echoes are found constantly in Titian's paintings. One magnificent tragic example occurs in the "Entombment" in the Louvre (fig. 3), where the limp arm of the dead Christ is repeated in a fold of checkered scarf, and this, crumpled as it falls to the ground, ends in a small mass that in shape and action is like Christ's hand. Such formal likenesses remind one of simile and metaphor in poetry, and they might be called *pictorial metaphors*. It has been said that the force of a metaphor depends on sensuous nearness and logical farness. It is easily seen how this principle applies in the present instances.

The main features of a painting like the "Europa" were in the first place fairly well worked out by means of preliminary sketches and drawings, something like the one for an earlier composition shown in fig. 4, since no extensive revisions could be made in the painting itself without loss of quality. But, opposed to the minute following of details in a precisely defined drawing, as in earlier practice, Titian, especially in his seventies or eighties when this picture was painted, had developed a new and freer procedure (to be discussed more fully later) which enabled him

3. TITIAN: Entombment

to think out many of the details of his compositions as he went along. According to accounts of contemporaries, he often took a long time, sometimes years, to complete his paintings — the "Europa," worked at along with other pictures, was apparently in hand for some two years — and the final touches were the result of prolonged study. In 1559 the Spanish secretary Hernandez wrote to Philip II to explain a delay in the delivery of two other paintings (the "Actaeon" and the "Callisto," now in the collection of Lord Ellesmere), saying that Titian needed twenty more days to finish the paintings because he wanted to do some "little things" to them which, according to Hernandez, "no one else would notice." It is not surprising, therefore, that today one frequently comes on new delights in the way of relationships which at first escaped observation.

4. TITIAN: Study for painting of The Jealous Husband in Scuola del Santo, Padua

PICTORIAL FORM

WHILE the development or expansion of theme accounts for much of the harmony and grandeur of the whole conception, it was necessarily accompanied by a consideration of the arrangement of the composition within the limits defined by the enclosing enframement.

In music thematic material is usually developed within the limits of certain definite structures known as musical forms, like sonata, minuet, rondo, and so on. In a similar way in painting there are certain structural arrangements which might be called *pictorial forms*. Although these have never been classified or defined so precisely as in music, they nevertheless may be thought of as separate and distinct arrangements which have been used, more or less consciously, from the Renaissance to our own day. The particular form employed in any individual case depended on appropriateness to the specific subject matter as well as on the general tradition within which the artist worked.

Before considering the composition of the "Europa" from this point of view, it may be helpful to explain a little more fully what is meant by the term, pictorial form, by referring to various examples. One simple and obvious form consists simply in placing a figure, object, or mass against a background comfortably within the enclosing outline, as in much ornamental design and as shown in painting in figs. 5 and 6. In the latter example the figures make a compact mass that repeats the squarish shape of the enframement, only turned at an angle of forty-five degrees. For subjects like the Madonna and Child or the Holy Family, Renaissance painters constantly employed the familiar pyramidal form (fig. 7). In altarpieces the composition usually assumed the symmetrical form of the traditional ceremony of Madonna and Saints itself. (fig. 8). For informal subject matter, especially where there was much action, any exact symmetry was felt to be inappropriate. Yet it is surprising how often in Venetian painting of the sixteenth century, in subjects not symmetrical in themselves, a suggestion of symmetry in the over-all pattern, or at least some strong accent

21

5. TITIAN: St. Sebastian

6. RUBENS: Rape of the Daughters of Leucippus

7. RAPHAEL: Holy Family

8. GIORGIONE: Madonna and Saints. Chiesa di San Liberale Abbaziale

9. TITIAN: Bacchanal (The Andrians)

10. TITIAN: Bacchus and Ariadne

on the vertical axis, is obtained to secure definite relation to the symmetry of the enframement. In any case, whether the composition be symmetrical or asymmetrical as far as spatial arrangement goes, there must be a balance of attractions of tone or color contrasts on either side of the vertical axis if there is to be a satisfactory feeling of equilibrium that harmonizes with the order of the outline. This of course is often a very subtle affair.

To illustrate a form used in many Venetian paintings of the earlier sixteenth century one may take Titian's "Bacchus and Ariadne" in the National Gallery in London (fig. 10), in which the underlying structure is based simply on the vertical and the horizontal axis of the enclosing rectangle. The figures and setting are presented to the observer as in a ballet on the stage with the frame of the painting as proscenium. Leaving aside all the interest of the lively subject matter and considering only the formal arrangement, one finds the center, where the vertical and horizontal axes cross, marked by especially strong contrasts of light against dark and dark against light. Below, exactly on the vertical axis, is a small but striking accent in the form of a white blossom of the caper vine. With legs symmetrically astride this struts the small satyr, while the dog's head and paws on one side, and the calf's head and ears on the other, carry out still further a symmetrical pattern which fades out above in the leg of the Bacchante and the hind leg of the leopard in vague correspondence on either side. This bit of symmetry marking the vertical axis in the midst of the apparent confusion of the action is of the utmost value in helping to bring the whole design into harmony with the enframement.

The horizontal axis of the picture is indicated by the arm of Bacchus as well as by the head of Ariadne on one side and the head of the satyr on the other. It may also be observed that, as found over and over again in paintings by Titian and other Venetian masters, the distance of landscape and sky occupies roughly the upper left quarter of the whole area, and that the broken screen of trees on the opposite side comes over to the central axis to mark this division still further. When one considers that along with this formal arrangement, including metaphorical echoes [1] like those in the "Europa," the action all had to be ordered in a three-dimensional space involving a sequence extending from left foreground to extreme distance of sky and cloud, it seems that as if by some miracle everything had suddenly floated into a pattern of measures and shapes, quite independent of the representation but belonging to the geometry of the enclosing outline.

28

PICTORIAL FORM

The "Bacchus and Ariadne" was painted for the Duke of Ferrara to complete a series of pictures by Bellini, Dosso Dossi, and Titian, which served as decorations for a small room or *camerino* in the duke's palace, and it was evidently intended as a companion to the "Bacchanal" (or more specifically "The Andrians") now in Madrid (fig. 9). The trees and sky are reversed to suggest a balanced opposition in the two pictures taken together. In the "Bacchanal" the vertical and horizontal axes are not so clearly marked, but the essential form is the same. There is a similar accenting of the center by a strong contrast of dark against light, and a similar suggestion of symmetry on the vertical axis in the arrangement of figures in the lower part of the composition. But here the place of the caper blossom is taken by a small sheet of paper bearing the words and notes of a bit of song that gives the theme of the composition: "Qui boyt et ne reboyt/ Il ne scet que boyr soit."

The pictorial form employed in these paintings is typical of Titian's earlier work. In the "Europa" quite a different form is employed, one which is characteristic of the later sixteenth century. In this painting two overlapping, or interknit, structural schemes are played together. First, the composition is divided into two similar but inverted areas by the suggestion of a line that cuts across the whole area on a diagonal. If one imagines a line drawn from a little less than a foot (about one eighth of the total height of the picture) below the upper-right corner to a point the same distance above the lower-left corner, one finds that the main foreground part of the composition, including Europa and the bull and the Amor on the dolphin, comes in the lower-right section and the background of landscape and sky in the upper-left section. Europa's knee, strongly accented

---

[1] A few of these echoes or metaphors may be briefly noted. For instance, the mass of drapery flying from the shoulder of Bacchus is paralleled in much the same size by the branch of foliage above. The likeness is particularly clear if one turns the photograph upside down. This reveals the importance of the little patch of white cloud which accents the dark of the foliage, just as the light of the drapery snaps out the dark of Bacchus's head. The direction of these two masses is the significant one of the diagonal of the upper half of the whole picture. The lower outline of the foliage repeats the upper outline of the drapery.

The main mass of the figure of Ariadne, with the small loop of dress over her arm at the right, is echoed in the arrangement of the cloud above — larger mass and small loop to the right. A small curved mass of foliage above the Bacchante's cymbal repeats the gesture of her raised arm. And so on. This may suggest something of the huge amount of interknit relationships which, though impossible of complete analysis, produce the extraordinary richness of the final effect.

in the center of the composition against the sky, is thrust boldly upward so that its upper edge helps to define the diagonal line.[2] This is one of the pictorial forms based on an emphasis on a diagonal of the area which, with variations, came into extensive use in the later sixteenth century as particularly appropriate for informal subject matter.

Playing in with this diagonal cross-cutting is the suggestion of another form in which a V-shaped arrangement is used. In paintings in this form the V is usually upright as in Titian's early "Three Ages" in the Earl of Ellesmere's collection (fig. 11). In this the figures of the foreground are placed in the triangles to right and left, while the landscape comes, rather precisely in this case, in the open area of the V. Freer variations occur in the "Education of Cupid" in the Borghese Gallery in Rome (fig. 12) and in the "Diana and Callisto" in the Earl of Ellesmere's collection (fig. 13). It is a kind of inversion of the more familiar pyramidal form. But in the "Europa" the V is turned sideways with the apex marked by the hand grasping the bull's horn. The arrangement seems only subtly suggested, at least until one becomes aware of it, as it is also in the "Diana and Callisto." The landscape comes in the open space of the V, while the enclosing lines, curved in this case, converge on Europa's hand, placed with geometric precision on the horizontal axis. The two schemes are thus played together in a kind of counterpoint. The convergence helps in the expression of movement, while the pull on the eye to the right which it produces is counterbalanced by the attraction of the distance on the left. This is assisted by a conspicuous streak of light on the sea that is graded toward the left, as well as by the small spot of red in the dress of one of the handmaidens which echoes the red of Europa's scarf.

Again one may question how far the artist consciously planned all this neat geometry. Design is such an instinctive and so complex an affair that

---

[2] It is sometimes dangerous to depend too much on the present aspect of a painting executed some four hundred years ago; for, aside from some natural changes in the paint itself, it has inevitably in passing from owner to owner been subjected to a certain amount of cleaning and varnishing and, as in this case, relining, or backing with new canvas. In the process some of the paint surface may have been abraded, and some of the original canvas may even have been cut off. In the present instance it is possible that there is a loss of an inch or so all round, but evidently not enough to alter the shape of the picture. As for the surface, there has been some slight loss by rubbing as has been noted. But, as paintings go, the "Europa" is generally considered to be in unusually good condition, for the *impasto* (or thickness of the detailed touches) has not been flattened down as sometimes happens when a picture has been subjected to ironing in the process of relining. It is fairly safe, therefore, to assume that we can see a very large part of Titian's original intention.

11. TITIAN: Three Ages

12. TITIAN: The Education of Cupid

13. TITIAN: Diana and Callisto

there can be no evidence of how it was done except in the work itself. But it certainly was no accident. To the artist at work such planning may seem to be simply what we think of as "feeling" — that a thing must go this way, not that way — with rational realization sometimes coming afterwards. However, all the artists of the Renaissance were accustomed to think in geometrical terms; this was necessary in architecture, and there were few painters who were not to some extent architects. It was of course required for sculptured and painted decoration, and there was little painting that was not in part decoration.

REPRESENTATION AND
PERFORMANCE — PHRASING

IN what has been written above emphasis on the development of theme and on underlying structure has in some ways put the cart before the horse, for a very large part of the interest found in a painting lies in the representation itself: the rendering of form and space, and the actual performance in the handling of the paint.

Interest in the formal or abstract factor in design sometimes obscures the fact that a primary pleasure we derive from drawing and painting (aside from the interest of content and the possible beauty of the objects represented) depends on our perception of the order embodied in the relationships of the various touches or strokes which define the form and action convincingly. This is the essence of the delight which, from prehistoric cave-painting down to our own day, has always been taken in representation itself. The organization involved has definite aesthetic significance. It is the complete relationship of touches from this point of view that endows the slightest sketch by a master with so much meaning and beauty and distinguishes it from the work of the lesser artist.[1]

At the time the "Europa" was painted Titian had been steadily working for some fifty or sixty years until the putting of his thoughts into strokes of paint must have seemed almost as easy as talking. But, although in this picture he has worked with what seems to be the utmost freedom and has used a broader and looser handling than in his earlier painting, there is really no less precision or subtlety. The procedure which he here employed had been developed in Venice, partly by himself, in the earlier years of

---

[1] It is worth noting that it was the feeling of reality produced by Titian's paintings that impressed the writers of the sixteenth and seventeenth centuries. Thus in Lodovico Dolce's *Diologo della pittura* of 1557 one finds: "Il vivo non è piu vivo" (Life itself is not more lifelike). Crowe and Cavalcaselle in *Titian: His Life and Times* quote other authors: "All that Titian's figures want is a voice; in all else they are nature itself" (M. A. Biondo, 1549); "He was the very mirror of nature, only that the mirror reflects whilst Titian creates" (Boschini, 1664).

the sixteenth century. One may assume that once having the design well in mind, and also put down on paper in the form of more or less finished sketches, he laid out the main arrangement of areas of light and dark on the medium brownish ground-tone of the coating with which the canvas was primed. This was done, probably in an oil medium of some kind, with an earth red, white, and black, and perhaps with an occasional use of yellow or brown. The lighter passages were gradually built up with a fairly heavy *impasto* (layer or touch of opaque paint), while the darks and the half-tones were comparatively thin. With the arrangement of relatively warm and cool tones — that is, reds and yellows opposed to neutral grays which appeared slightly bluish by contrast — this gave a fairly complete effect, and only later were the cool grays reinforced in places with glazes or scumbles (thin or dragged layers of opaque paint) of the necessary blues and greens. Over this building up of the main forms Titian then worked out the final details and accents, but always, apparently, with periods of laying the picture aside, perhaps turned face to the wall (a practice described by his pupil Palma Giovane and recorded by the seventeenth-century writer, Boschini) in order to come back to it again with a fresh look.

As it happens, an illustration of this general procedure may be seen in an unfinished painting by Tintoretto in the Fogg Art Museum in Cambridge (fig. 14). It was painted probably some fifteen or twenty years after the "Europa" and reveals the more rapid manner of execution that was characteristic of Tintoretto's work. It is carried to near completion in the upper part, but the lower part shows only the first blocking in of the main masses of light and dark with a few bold strokes. The form of the legs is only briefly indicated to give a framework over which the dress was later to have been completed.

It is evident that Titian's painting, in spite of the illusion of reality it produced, is completely different in aim and method from any "naturalistic" painting of later times intended to give the actual appearance of things and painted directly from the scene. Constantly Titian's handling of space and effect of light is a matter of abstract and arbitrary convention. Thus the expression of form is assisted to some extent by differences in the thickness of the paint surface; the lights, especially in the flesh tones, are usually built up in a heavy impasto, which assists in the expression of flesh texture. The expression of existence in space depends particularly on the variation of contrasts and the treatment of edges. In general, strong

14. TINTORETTO: Allegory of Fidelity

contrasts and sharp edges tend to come forward, and lesser contrasts and softer edges to recede. The expression of light effect is often quite arbitrary. For example, the raised arm of Europa is shown against the mass of the scarf; but, with little regard for any actual lighting, to give the arm existence in space the contrasts of the folds are suppressed where they come close to the arm, while the main mass comes out more strongly lighted and with stronger contrasts in order to hold its place in turn against the subdued contrasts of the sky. Likewise, beyond the relatively strong contrasts in the raised knee, those in the sky are extremely subdued. The stronger contrasts of the landscape are kept well away from the figure. As another instance, one may note the way in which the lower leg is given existence in front of the drapery on the bull's back by a sharp edge of dark against the lightening of the folds below, while above, the light on the knee comes against a line of arbitrary dark. As a conventional means of expressing space this is almost as abstract as that of Chinese ink painting.[2]

In this connection one should take note of Titian's exploitation of the expressive possibilities of shadow. For example, take the brilliant and daring piece of invention involved in the throwing of the dark shadow across the face of Europa. As well as assisting in the suggestion of existence in three dimensions, it adds enormously to the sense of dramatic tension. Of course in all Venetian painting of the sixteenth century composition depended largely on the opposition of masses of light and shadow. As opposed to the suggestion of sculptured relief in earlier painting, this was an essential part of the Venetian mode of representation. But it was Titian who played a large part in its development. No one before him had thought of placing the head of a principal figure in shadow, as he did, perhaps experimentally and not altogether successfully, in an early altarpiece ("St. Mark and other Saints," now in the Salute in Venice), and as he did with assurance in the "Entombment" (fig. 3). In the latter the tragic effect is enhanced by the placing of the head of Christ into deep shadow against the light of dawn in the sky.

That this mode of representation, in spite of its strong plastic feeling, is not at all a realistic rendering of spatial effect is seen immediately if one considers the effect of space achieved by quite other means in the "Concert" by Vermeer, in the Dutch Room of the Museum. In the "Europa," despite the suggestion of veiled sunlight, the modeling of the different fields into shadow fails to follow any realistic law of diminution of contrasts on which the natural effect in the Vermeer depends. Titian was thus able, notwithstanding the abstract illusion of space, to keep something of the feeling of tapestry-like decoration. That the picture was considered decoration in this sense is witnessed by its adoption by Velazquez for the design of a tapestry in the background of his painting, "The Tapestry Weavers," in the Prado in Madrid.

The abstract character of the representation is witnessed also by the fact

[2] This is discussed more fully in Arthur Pope, *The Language of Drawing and Painting* (Cambridge, 1949).

38

15. TITIAN: Venus and Cupid

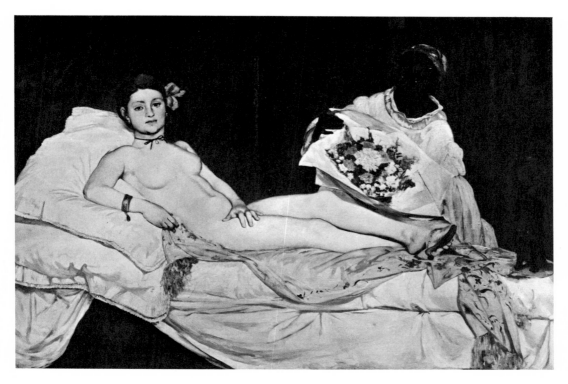

16. MANET: Olympia

that we are not at all disturbed by the arbitrary arrangement from the point of view of perspective. In the rendering of the figures of Europa and the bull the eye level of the observer cannot be supposed to be more than a few feet above the surface of the sea; but we look down on the distressed maidens on the shore from a considerable height. Here it goes without notice, but such a lapse, or rather convenient disregard of literal fact, would in the Vermeer be painfully conspicuous. Moreover, there would probably be difficulty in analyzing the anatomical structure of the figure of Europa to satisfy a jury of academic artists of the nineteenth century (Michelangelo was of course critical of Titian's drawing); or in justifying her precarious pose from the point of view of gravity, which Titian, without any sacrifice of illusion, seems constantly to have flouted. In the "Venus and Cupid" in the Uffizi (fig. 15), for example, the figure seems to float rather than to exert any pressure on the supporting couch; otherwise it would have been impossible to preserve the long classical curve of the thigh. In such paintings the pose is a mental concept, quite unlike a literal rendering of the pose of an actual reclining figure, exhibited in striking contrast by Manet's "Olympia" (fig. 16).

As pointed out above, the procedure involved in this way of painting provided a foundation for the rendering of final details of form with rather free superimposed touches of opaque paint or transparent glazes. The reproductions of details in the plates give some idea of the fresh quality of the performance in this last step of the whole procedure, and, although photographic reproductions inevitably miss many of the more delicate distinctions of light and dark, they give at least some notion of its subtlety. In this connection one may recall Ruskin's dictum that "all great art is delicate."

The reproductions may also give an idea of what may appropriately be called *phrasing*. This is very similar to what is meant by phrasing in music, where it seems to be the final factor that distinguishes the performance of the true virtuoso. In painting it refers especially to the ordered variation of sizes, shapes, tones, and intervals, so that each detail and each group of details has its individual character and place in the larger order of the whole design. This is opposed to the mannered monotony of touch so apt to be seen in the work of commonplace artists.[3] It is difficult to deal with this in words alone; one needs to be able to point with one's finger or a stick. But at least something may be done to illustrate what is meant by this factor.

REPRESENTATION AND PERFORMANCE

Take the rendering of the bull's horn described by Ovid: "perfect in shape as if carved by an artist's hand." Each touch has its individual size, shape, and tone, not exactly like any other, and also its unique position within a sequence of touches, graded in size, tone, and spacing, which not only describes the form but gives delight as abstract design. Or observe the graded strokes which define the scales of the dolphin, or the grouped lights on the Amor's wings, or the strokes which describe his golden locks. Look at the bull's eyebrow, and then lower down at the curving strokes which indicate the ripples of the water; or at the accents in the dolphin's eye and the delicately graded touches which indicate the teeth of the fabulous-appearing monster in the extreme foreground.[4]

It is clear that Titian's thought has gone into every touch and has been accompanied by perfect control of the brush. Each touch and phrase has definite meaning and adds its indispensable bit to the total quantity of interest and order; at the same time it is kept in its proper place in relation to the larger masses and to the whole design. The superficial appearance of loose handling is thus deceptive. This is very different from a mere dabbing in of light accents, as lesser painters have sometimes done, in an attempt to spark up a dull foundation into a specious brilliance. With Titian it is the sheer quantity of orderly relationships which produces the richness of effect. It is his masterly control which gives his work such a definite classic quality. This is exhibited very clearly in the book by John Walker, *Bellini*

---

[3] How the subtleties of this phrasing are accomplished in musical performance is described by Homer W. Smith in the chapter on Consciousness in his book, *From Fish to Philosopher* (Boston, 1953). In contrasting the interpretation of a fine pianist with the relative automatism of the inferior performer, which approaches that of the mechanical piano, he writes: "The artist achieves his interpretation by minute deviations from uniformity and regularity: one note is held longer than the metronome permits, another is hurried; one note is struck firmly, another only lightly touched; a succession of notes each having equal paper value may be played with uneven tonal emphasis, or slurred deliberately, or made to parade in a presumptuous or sensuous manner" (p. 197).

Change of only a few words is needed to make this description apply to what happens in painting. One thinks immediately of Titian, of dragged brush strokes, of sharp accents, of Veronese, of Velazquez. A visitor to the Museum might well look at the painting of the gold chain in Rubens' portrait of the Earl of Arundel in the Dutch Room.

One thinks also of what happens when a painting is copied by an inferior artist. The copy may reproduce the picture's main design fairly well; but there is all the difference in the world between the performance of the master and that of the copyist.

[4] Not really fabulous, but a perfectly good live Adriatic fish painted with complete understanding of its structure — according to Professor Henry B. Bigelow of the Museum of Comparative Zoology at Harvard. On being shown a photograph of this and of the head of the supposed dolphin, Mr. Bigelow exclaimed that Titian ought to have been an ichthyologist.

17. RUBENS: Free Copy of Titian's Bacchanal

18. TITIAN: Bacchanal (The Andrians)

and Titian at Ferrara, in which, to illustrate the difference between the northern Baroque taste of the seventeenth century and that of the Venetian Renaissance of the sixteenth century, reproductions of the "Venus Worship" and the "Bacchanal" by Titian and of the free copies, or really variations, made by Rubens are shown side by side. The comparison is so illuminating that (with acknowledgment to Mr. Walker) the original painting of the "Bacchanal" and the version by Rubens now in Stockholm are here shown also side by side (figs. 17 and 18). Compared with the loose and fluid transformation produced by Rubens, the strict order and classic finality of the Titian is startling.

COLOR

THE painting certainly produces an effect of rich color; and yet, like so many paintings by other Venetian masters always thought of as great colorists, it contains no really intense color. The stronger contrasts are mostly of light and dark, and color is mainly a matter of opposition of warm and cool tones. Although these tones are for the most part surprisingly subdued, the effect is at the same time lively and sparkling. This is due to the play of crisp touches that are constantly and subtly varied. It is particularly notable in the mass of red and pinkish scarf with its sharp-edged accents of pale gold lights. Hues are limited to a range from red, which is hardly more than the red-orange of Venetian red, through yellow to green and blue. There is no suggestion of the violet region of the spectrum (or color circle). One receives a suggestion of bright color in the pinkish tone of the scarf, and this of course was intended; but it is all relative. Small accents on the wings of the *Amorini* look almost like vermilion, but they are actually only the earth red of other passages. Did not Degas once remark that the business of the painter is to use Venetian red, but to make it look like vermilion?

To refer again to music, one often receives a feeling of great richness and volume of sound from orchestral passages in which, if measured in decibels, it is not actually very great — less in fact than in many compositions where extra instruments are brought in to make more and greater variety of sound. The richness of color in the "Europa" might be thought of as an illusion produced by similar means. From this point of view the visitor to the Museum may compare the "Europa" with the painting ("The Child Jesus Disputing in the Temple") by Titian's pupil, Paris Bordone, which hangs on the opposite wall. In the latter picture an attempt to give interest by a greater variety of color has produced a relatively spotty effect, as opposed to the more closely knit unity of the "Europa."

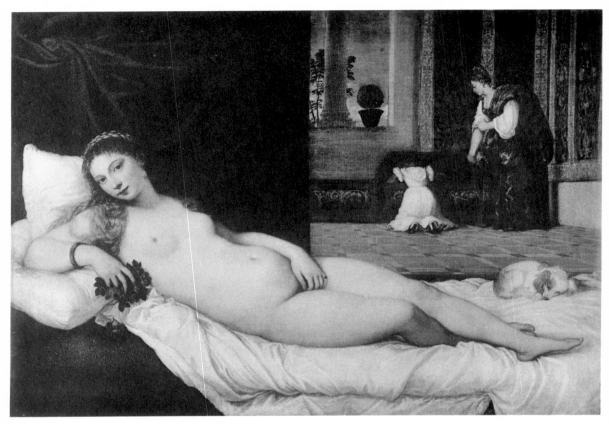

19. TITIAN: Venus of Urbino

20. PALMA VECCHIO: Venus

PICTORIAL FORM IN
RELATED PAINTINGS

IT may interest the reader to consider the matter of pictorial form in connection with certain other paintings since this is a subject not often touched upon. Thus the form based on the vertical and horizontal axes employed in the "Bacchus and Ariadne" and the "Bacchanal" is exhibited more obviously in other paintings by Titian as well as in some by other artists of the sixteenth century.

Titian's so-called "Venus of Urbino" in the Uffizi Gallery in Florence is a striking example (fig. 19). The general pattern of the whole picture occurs also in the "Venus" by Palma Vecchio (1480–1528) in the Dresden Gallery (fig. 20) and also, surprisingly enough, in the "Warrior Adoring the Christ Child," attributed to Catena (d. 1531) — though possibly also by Palma — in the National Gallery in London (fig. 21). In the two Venus subjects the division by vertical and horizontal axes in the background seems to stabilize the design; the figure is placed in the foreground against this framework and is divided from it by a diagonal cross-cutting. In the Palma the elbow marks the horizontal axis. Palma's "Venus" was painted before Titian's, and they both derive from the earlier "Venus" by Giorgione now in Dresden; but since this was left unfinished by him and completed by Titian, and then altered by repainting, we do not know what was originally intended for its complete design. Titian's later painting of "Venus and Cupid" in the Uffizi (fig. 15) is another variation of the form used in his earlier work, but it exhibits a freer use of sweeping curves to give a feeling of harmony by the repetition of a specific shape character.

These Venus paintings served as models for other artists who frequently adapted the same pattern and form to slightly different subject matter. Amusing and very German variations were made by Lucas Cranach (1472–1553). One of these, the "Nymph of the Spring" in Leipzig, is shown in fig. 22. Another entertaining adaptation is seen in a "Cleopatra" by the

21. CATENA: Warrior Adoring Christ Child

Dutch master, Scorel (fig. 23), in which, although the pictorial form is Venetian, the shape character of the details is completely Dutch.

Veronese's garden-party-like version of the subject of Europa in the Ducal Palace in Venice (fig. 24) also depends on a framework of vertical and horizontal axes; but the group of figures on the left is built up into an almost perfectly symmetrical pattern, with the axis marked by Europa's foot. This use of symmetry as a means of organizing an off-center group, while still keeping an informal arrangement, is a device used frequently in the later sixteenth and in the seventeenth century — by Poussin, for instance.

Among the many variations of the scheme of diagonal cross-cutting noted in the design of Titian's "Europa," Veronese's "Alexander and the Family of Darius" in the National Gallery in London (fig. 25) may be taken as a particularly clear example, though even here there is actually a playing together of two different schemes. The architecture forms a background of verticals and horizontals and the large mass comes on the central axis to emphasize the central position of the principal figures in the drama, while there is also a less strongly accented division into fourths. The cross-cutting

22. CRANACH: Nymph of the Spring

23. VAN SCOREL: Cleopatra

24. VERONESE: The Rape of Europa

comes here on the actual diagonal of the rectangle. The line of cross-cutting is of course more or less broken to conform to the action, but the main mass of figures, embracing strong contrasts and generally darker tones than those of the background (contrasts are exaggerated in the photograph), comes in the lower-right section and the lighter tones of architecture and so on in the upper-left. When minor dark areas encroach on the larger light area, corresponding lighter accents are introduced — across the center — into the darker section.

Composition based on diagonal cross-cutting has been referred to here as a distinct pictorial form which painters came to use as one way of or-

25. VERONESE: Alexander and the Family of Darius

ganizing certain types of material. Other examples might be cited from the sixteenth, seventeenth, or eighteenth centuries. But it may be more interesting to show an adaptation of the same fundamental form in a more recent work, like the pastel by Degas in the Hill-Stead Museum in Farmington, Conn. (fig. 26). The diagonal cutting is from the upper to the lower edge of the outline, but it is essentially the same form as that of the "Europa." Relative foreground comes in the right section containing the figure, and relative distance in the left, while subordinate accents, as is common in this form, give correspondence across the center instead of on either side of the vertical axis. In passing one may note echoes of shapes surprisingly Titianesque in character: the curve of the hips repeated in the round of the tub, and the way in which the curtains touch the floor to suggest a likeness to the feet. The comparison of Degas with Titian may seem strange,[1] for certainly Degas' woman is no goddess and the picture has no content aside from the beauty of the thing seen. But, after all, a large part of the excellence in Degas' design, like the expression of space in Cezanne's painting, derives from his study and understanding of earlier European painting, and he occupies a place among those who continued the best of the main European tradition to the end of the nineteenth century.

[1] "The only basis for true comparison, Plato says, is the excellence that is peculiar to each thing." Edith Hamilton, *The Greek Way* (New York, 1930), p. 138.

26. DEGAS: Femme au Tub

NOTE ON TITIAN'S LIFE

SINCE this small book is intended simply to call attention to some of the distinguishing qualities of a particular painting, there is need here for only a few brief remarks on Titian's life and his work as a whole. For anyone desiring further information, some of the more helpful of the enormous number of books and articles that have been written about Titian will be found in the list of books suggested for reference.

The second edition of the famous "Lives" by the painter-historian Giorgio Vasari (1511–1571), published in 1568, contains the following passage: "In the year 1566, when Vasari, the writer of the present History, was at Venice, he went to visit Titian, as one who was his friend, and found him, although then very old, still with pencil in his hand and painting busily. Great pleasure had Vasari in beholding his works and in conversation with the master."

"Painting busily" was what Titian had been doing for not far short of a century. That was his real life, and the record of it is to be found only in his paintings, in a few engravings after his designs, and in a small number of drawings which by good fortune have been preserved.

As for the facts of his other, or outward, life, his real name was Tiziano Vecelli, and he was born in Pieve di Cadore, a small town in that still most beautiful country in the hills and mountains beyond the plain to the north of Venice. Throughout his life he is said to have paid yearly visits to Pieve, and the trees, hills, mountains, church towers, castles, and the rustic farm buildings with shepherds and their flocks, supplied the motives for the landscape which forms an important feature of so many of his paintings. He died in Venice in 1576; but the date of his birth remains uncertain. In a letter to Philip II written in 1571, he describes himself as ninety-five years of age, and, according to this, he would have been born in 1476 or 1477. However, recent authorities believe this to have been a mistake and, on the basis of other evidence, place the date of his birth some ten years later. With reference to the "Europa" it makes little difference whether it was painted when he was in his seventies or his eighties, for our main concern is with the fact that it was based on the visual experience and the practice of painting of well over sixty years.

Coming at an early age to Venice he soon entered the workshop of Giovanni Bellini (1430?–1516), the leading Venetian painter of the late fifteenth and the early sixteenth century. It was there that he learned his craft, probably over a period of some years. Among his fellow pupils were Sebastiano Luciani (c.1485–1547), later known as "del Piombo," and Palma Vecchio (1480–1528), as well as Giorgione (1478–1510) who soon became the dominant spirit of this younger group of painters. Giorgione took the lead in transforming the gentle religious sentiment of Bellini into a romantic lyrical style which recaptured much of the spirit of classical pastoral and love poetry. The others followed this style, or fashion, as closely as they could, including even the master Bellini himself, though his aged attempts, as in the "Feast of the Gods" (now in the National Gallery in Washington), remained a bit stilted. Classical themes were used as motives for paintings frankly pagan in spirit, while even religious subjects like Holy Families, or Madonnas with a saint or two, became pleasant picnics in the country. The different painters of this new generation were for the moment all so Giorgionesque that it often puzzles modern critics to determine just who was responsible for one or another picture.[1] The problem is still further complicated by the fact that Titian is known to have completed some of Giorgione's paintings which had been left unfinished on the latter's untimely death of plague in 1510.

Following the death of Giorgione, Titian soon proved himself to be the best of this group of younger painters, and, although his peculiar dramatic power was not revealed until the completion of the large "Assumption" for the church of the Frari in 1518, after the death of Bellini in 1516 he became recognized as the most distinguished painter of Venice and indeed, before long, of all Europe. His reputation was enhanced by the completion in 1523 of the series of works undertaken for the decoration of the Duke of Ferrara's *camerino*. These included the "Worship of Venus," the "Bacchanal," and the "Bacchus and Ariadne," and also the repainting of

---

[1] For example, in Hendy's *Catalogue of the Exhibited Paintings and Drawings* of the Gardner Museum, the painting of "Christ Bearing the Cross," believed by most critics to be the work of Giorgione, is attributed by Hendy to Palma Vecchio. The "Concert Champêtre" in the Louvre presents a similar problem. The use of shadow and of metaphorical echoes favor Titian as at least part author.

a large portion of Bellini's "Feast of the Gods" to bring it more into harmony with his own pictures in the same room.

From now on commissions poured in not only from the citizens of Venice, as witnessed by the great Pesaro Altarpiece of 1526 in the Frari, but also from the most prominent figures of the time, including the Emperor Charles V and, in due course, his son King Philip II, Pope Paul III, the Dukes of Ferrara, Mantua, and Urbino, and many lesser lights who were willing to pay for his services. These commissions varied from altarpieces for the churches to allegories, mythological subjects, and portraits for the houses and palaces. By the Emperor, after the completion of the portrait painted in Bologna in 1533, Titian was created Count Palatine and Knight of the Golden Spur, and he achieved an honored and dignified position in society rare among the artists of the time.

Much of the record of the middle portion of Titian's life is taken up with his professional or "business" trips, to Ferrara, Bologna, Mantua, Urbino, and so on, finally to Rome in 1545–46, and to Augsburg in 1548 and again in 1550. On his visit to Rome he met Michelangelo, Vasari, and other artists, and he saw the paintings of Raphael and Michelangelo. He seems to have been particularly interested in the antiquities which were shown to him by Vasari and which he was able to see in greater quantity and variety than had been possible in Venice and Padua. Without doubt, when painting a subject like the "Europa," he had in the back of his mind recollections of classical sculpture. The *putti,* the dolphins, the floating scarf, and even to some extent the general arrangement and the plastic quality in the rendering of the form recall late classical reliefs. Like other artists of the Renaissance, although his approach was less theoretical than that of the scientific Florentines, and although "the atmosphere of a picture by Titian is not that which one breathes in a museum of antiquities," [2] still Titian in his treatment of the human figure depended almost as much on the antique as on the live model.

Although these occasional journeys were necessary, mostly for the painting of portraits, he much preferred to remain in Venice where he had his painting materials, his assistants, and his models ready at hand. Here, also, in his large house on the northern side of the island, with its garden running to the waterside and looking across to Murano and the hills and mountains

---

[2] "L'atmosphere d'un tableau de Titien n'est celle qui se respire dans un musée d'antiques." Louis Hourticq, *La Jeunesse de Titien* (Paris, 1919), p. 160.

of Cadore, he could relax with his family and entertain his friends. Among the latter were the sculptor Jacopo Sansovino (1486–1570) and the writer Pietro Aretino (1492–1556), who, with Titian, formed what was known as the triumvirate. Much of our knowledge of Titian's activities is derived from Aretino's letters, some of which reveal him almost in the guise of Titian's publicity agent. "Titian has been always healthy and happy," wrote Vasari; "he has been favoured beyond the lot of most men, and has received from Heaven only favours and blessings. In his house he has been visited by whatever Princes, Literati, or men of distinction have gone to or dwelt in Venice; for, to say nothing of his excellence in art he has always distinguished himself by courtesy, goodness, and rectitude."

Titian's immediate family included his brother Francesco, also a painter; his wife Cecilia, who died in 1530; his sons Pomponio, a ne'er-do-well, and Orazio; his daughter Lavinia; and his sister Orsa, who, on the death of Cecilia, came to look after his house. His son Orazio seems to have become his principal assistant and, toward the end of his life, second-in-command of what became a typical Renaissance workshop. Numerous pupils and assistants were employed not only to help in the painting of details of costume, landscape, and so on, in the usual way, but to turn out copies or versions of the more popular of their master's works according to demand. These were probably in many cases painted partly by Titian himself, and they naturally add to the difficulties of modern criticism in making distinctions between the work of the master and that of "the school." Orazio died of the plague in 1576, apparently shortly before Titian's own death. The workshop, or "firm," thus came to an end. Not long after, the worthless Pomponio sold the house and its contents.

In considering Titian's work as a whole it is easy to suspect that the presence of certain defects or inconsistencies in some of his paintings was due to the collaboration of assistants. On the other hand, his compositions were not always entirely successful; he lacked the skill of Veronese in handling subjects with large numbers of figures. He was at his best in moderate-sized canvases, especially in those which seem to have been painted entirely by his own hand.

There is a wonderful health and sanity in Titian's attitude toward his art which is without any suggestion of conscious self-expression. One thinks of what Gilbert Murray must have had in mind when he said, "The artist ought to be thinking of his subject and his work, and not of himself at all." [3]

Titian's dramatic power, like that of Giotto or of Rembrandt, depended on his ability to project himself imaginatively into his subject and into the feelings of his different characters in the manner of a good actor, so that even the slightest gesture seems to be the spontaneous result of inner thought or emotion. This is evident in his portraits which in this respect have never been surpassed. In contrast, one may turn to the scientific Leonardo, the action of whose figures often appears the result of calculation from the outside. This is not to disparage Leonardo's more rational attitude — his interests and aims were of a different kind from Titian's, and they were more complex. Titian was, more simply, just a painter.

---

[3] *The Classical Tradition in Poetry,* The Charles Eliot Norton Lectures (Cambridge, 1927), p. 243.

HISTORY OF THE PAINTING

IN a number of letters written by Titian to Philip II between June 1559 and April 1562, published in 1877 by Crowe and Cavalcaselle in *Titian: His Life and Times*, there is mention of the "Europa" as being in hand. The last of these, dated 26 April 1562, runs as follows:

Most serene and Catholic King:

With the help of Divine Providence I have at last finished the two pictures already begun for your Catholic Majesty. One is the "Christ praying in the Garden," the other the "Poesy of Europa carried by the Bull," both of which I send, and I may say that these put the seal on all that your Majesty was pleased to order and I bound to deliver on various occasions.

Devoted humble servant

Titian.

(The original Italian text of this and the other letters is given by Crowe and Cavalcaselle in their appendix.)

What happened after this is told by Hendy in the *Catalogue of Exhibited Paintings and Drawings* of the Gardner Museum:

There remained the mere matter of payment, for which Titian was still asking in a letter of 22 December 1574. The Europa portata dal toro appears fifth in a list he encloses of pictures painted for the King.

The Poesie hung in the royal palace in Madrid and became perhaps something of an embarrassment in the seventeenth century, when the Renaissance was losing its convictions. Descending through Philip III, they were given away by Philip IV to the Prince of Wales, later King Charles I. King Philip had been dangling the hand of his sister the Infanta Maria across what he thought the safety of the seas without any intention of actually bestowing it on a Protestant. When in the early spring of 1623 the Prince and the favourite Buckingham appeared unannounced in Madrid to see and carry off the bride, there was consternation, and the Europa was one of the courteous gifts intended as a substitute for the Princess. But the English were as unwilling to receive a Catholic queen. The Prince was recalled to England so precipitately that he had to leave his presents, ready packed as they were, in Madrid. King Charles never succeeded in obtaining them, and Philip eventually avenged the embarrassment upon him by buying after Charles' execution all his pictures that he could, including Mantegna's Santa Conversazione *now also in the Museum. Descending through Charles II of Spain to Philip V, the first Bourbon King, the* Europa *was given by him early in the eighteenth century to the Duc de Grammont, from whom it passed into the collection of the Duc d'Orléans, Regent of France (d. 1723), who was the owner of the little panel,* The Pietà, *by Raphael. They hung in the Palais Royal in Paris until his great-grandson "Philippe Egalité" sold the collection to an English syndicate formed of the Duke of Bridgewater, the Earl of Carlisle and Earl Gower, later the Marquis of Stafford. Each kept a picture gallery for himself, and the remainder was dispersed in sales in London by their agent Bryan. The* Europa *was sold 7 May 1804 (Peter Coxe, Burrell and Foster, "Mr. Bryan's Celebrated Gallery of Original Pictures of the Very First Importance," No. 47) to Bettesworth (marked catalogue in the Museum). It was in the collections of the Earl of Berwick and then of the Earl of Darnley at Cobham Hall (before 1824). From the Earl of Darnley Dr. von Bode had hoped to obtain it for the Kaiser Friedrich Museum but it was bought by Mrs. Gardner in June 1896 through Berenson, who wrote of it 10 May from Rome.*

BOOKS SUGGESTED FOR REFERENCE

Bernard Berenson, *The Venetian Painters of the Renaissance*. New York, 1894. Third edition, 1906.
Especially useful for a discussion of the general spirit underlying Venetian painting of the sixteenth century.

———— *Italian Pictures of the Renaissance*. Oxford, 1932. A list of artists and their works. Indispensable for the study of Italian painting. Illustrated edition: *The Venetian School*. 2 vols. London, 1957. 628 illustrations.

J. A. Crowe and G. B. Cavalcaselle, *Titian: His Life and Times*. 2 vols. London, 1877. Contains hitherto unpublished records and is the foundation for later works on Titian.

O. Fischel, *Tizian: Des Meisters Gemälde*. Fifth edition. Vol. 3 in *Klassiker der Kunst*. Berlin and Leipzig. 368 illustrations.

G. Gronau, *Titian*. London, 1904.

Detlev Freiherr von Hadeln, *Titian's Drawings*. London, 1927.

Philip Hendy, *Catalogue of the Exhibited Paintings and Drawings,* The Isabella Stewart Gardner Museum, Boston, 1931.

Louis Hourticq. *La Jeunesse de Titien*. Paris, 1919.

Charles Ricketts, *Titian*. London, 1910.

Hans Tietze, *Titian's Paintings and Drawings*. Second edition. London, 1950. 300 illustrations. Extensive bibliography.
A revision of the original German text in *Tizian: Leben und Werk*. 2 vols. Vienna, 1936.

E. Tietze-Conrat, "Titian's Workshop in his Late Years," *Art Bulletin,* XXVIII (June 1946).
An account of Titian's relation to his assistants.

John Walker, *Bellini and Titian at Ferrara*. London, 1956.

Listed below are the titles of some of the original sources of information concerning Titian's life and the history of his paintings.

L'Anonimo (thought to be Marcantonio Michiel), *Notizie d' opere di disegno.* Bassano, 1800. A more recent edition is G. C. Williamson, editor, *The Anonimo,* translated by Paolo Mussi. London, 1903.

A manuscript, discovered and published in 1800 by the Abate Don Jacopo Morelli. Written in the early sixteenth century, it contains notes, as if for a guidebook, on the objects of art in private houses, churches, and other buildings in Venice, Padua, and other towns in north Italy. If the collection in one of the Venetian houses like that of the Vendramini had remained intact and been added to in the following centuries, it would probably have presented much the same appearance as the collection now in the Gardner Museum. It is possible that Mrs. Gardner had something of this in mind in forming her collection.

Pietro Aretino, *Lettere.* 6 vols. Venice, 1537–1557. Later edition: Paris, 1609.

Marco Boschini, *Le Riche minere della pittura veneziana.* Venice, 1674.

Lodovico Dolce, *Diologo della pittura intitolato L'Aretino.* Venice, 1557.

Carlo Ridolfi, *Le Maraviglie dell' arte.* Venice, 1648.

Stefano Ticozzi, *Vite dei pittori Vecelli di Cadore.* Milan, 1817.

Giorgio Vasari, *Le Vite de' piu eccellenti pittori, scultori ed architettori.* Florence, 1555. Second edition, 1568. Edition Milanese: Florence, 1878–1882.

——— *Lives of Seventy of the Most Eminent Painters, Sculptors and Architects,* edited by E. H. and E. W. Blashfield. 4 vols. London, 1897.

A convenient edition containing the translations of Mrs. Jonathan Foster published in 1850.